Tor

Tor and the Deep Web: A Guide to Become Anonymous Online, Conceal Your IP Address, Block NSA Spying and Hack!

Joshua Welsh

The follow eBook is reproduced below with the goal of providing information that is as accurate and reliable as possible. Regardless, purchasing this eBook can be seen as consent to the fact that both the publisher and the author of this book are in no way experts on the topics discussed within and that any recommendations or suggestions that are made herein are for entertainment purposes only. Professionals should be consulted as needed prior to undertaking any of the action endorsed herein.

This declaration is deemed fair and valid by both the American Bar Association and the Committee of Publishers Association and is legally binding throughout the United States.

Furthermore, the transmission, duplication or reproduction of any of the following work including specific information will be considered an illegal act irrespective of if it is done electronically or in print. This extends to creating a secondary or tertiary copy of the work or a recorded copy and is only allowed with express written consent from the Publisher. All additional right reserved.

The information in the following pages is broadly considered to be a truthful and accurate account of facts and as such any inattention, use or misuse of the information in question by the reader will render any resulting actions solely under their purview. There are no scenarios in which the publisher or the original author of this work can be in any fashion deemed liable for any hardship or damages that may befall them after undertaking information described herein.

Additionally, the information in the following pages is intended only for informational purposes and should thus be thought of as universal. As befitting its nature, it is presented without assurance regarding its prolonged validity or interim quality. Trademarks that are mentioned are done without written consent and can in no way be considered an endorsement from the trademark holder.

Table of Contents

Introduction

Chapter one: Tor- What is it and How Can it Benefit You?.....1

Chapter two: Using Tor to Be Anonymous Online.................. 9

Chapter three: Browsing the Internet Anonymously with Tor

....12

Chapter four: Evading the NSA So They Cannot Spy on You18

Chapter five: Using Tor for Hacking.. 22

Chapter six: Types of Hacking..32

Chapter seven: Hacking into the Tor Network......................... 37

Chapter eight: The Weaknesses of Tor.................................... 47

Conclusion

Introduction

Congratulations on downloading *Tor* and thank you for doing so.

The following chapters will discuss how you will use Tor for more than just hiding who you are online. Tor can be used for hacking into programs without anyone seeing you.

Tor is going to be one of the programs that is sought after the most by the government and law offices everywhere despite the fact that you may not be using it for illegal activities. You will learn more about this in later chapters of the book.

There are plenty of books on this subject on the market, thanks again for choosing this one! Every effort was made to ensure it is full of as much useful information as possible, please enjoy!

Chapter one

TOR- WHAT IS IT AND HOW CAN IT BENEFIT YOU?

Tor is a program that is made up of a network of servers that are operated by teams of volunteers so that people are able to improve the security as well as the privacy that they have when it comes to them browsing online. Anyone who is using Tor is going to be connected through a series of virtual tunnels that are going to make it to where there is no direct connection to what they are doing and themselves. Therefore, when someone shares any sort of information on a public network, they are not going to need to worry about their privacy being compromised. It also makes it to where a user is allowed to access destinations that are normally restricted online.

It is necessary to use Tor when it comes to helping protect against online surveillance which is otherwise known as traffic analysis. Traffic analysis is used when someone is wanting to see what is being done on a public network. The different sources and destinations of the traffic that occurs on the internet gives other people a way to track someone's interests and behaviors which leads to making hacking easier because they know more about you than you know they do. People who do this are going to be making it difficult for you to be able to get a job if you are applying online or even affect your physical safety by figuring out exactly where you are located.

The internet collects data packets and when these packets are broken down, this is when traffic analysis comes into play. The payload that comes from the data along with the header is going to be what directs traffic whenever online. This payload is going to be the information that is embedded whenever emails, audio files, or webpages are accessed. While the payload will be encrypted, the traffic analysis is going to be able to expose most of this information so that what you are looking for online is exposed. The header is one focus of traffic analysis to because it lists the destination, source, timing, and size of the files found on the internet.

Whenever Tor is downloaded, the download process is simple because the only thing that needs to be downloaded is the Tor browser. After it has been downloaded, it can be used just like any other browser would be used. Tor is available on multiple operating systems as well. There is extra information on the Tor website that are going to assist in the process of using Tor.

After Tor has been downloaded, it can be used as soon as the download is done. Since Tor is one of the more secure browsers, there is going to be government intelligence agencies that are going to watch it. Surprisingly, the FBI has admitted that they have tried to take Tor down with a malware attack.

There are of course weaknesses with Tor, but it has yet to be completely penetrated. When Tor is used the way that it is supposed to be, then what you are doing online will be completely hidden from anyone spying on you.

When you use Tor correctly, your computer is going to have less of a chance of being compromised, but there are other things that you can do to make it even easier to protect yourself while using Tor.

> Tor should not be used on Windows. That includes using the Tor bundles. The bundles have weaknesses that were part of the takedown of Freedom Hosting by the FBI.

> If a workstation cannot be created when you are using Linux along with Tor, make sure that you have a proxy such as Privoxy along with a browser that has a firewall for any data that might leave the browser. If Clearnet is not working, try Tails or Whonix because they are going to help make sure that no data is leaked. There must be a firewall to make sur that no third party can get ahold of your data so that they can figure out where you are on the internet.

➤ Any sTorage that you are using needs to be encrypted. The most up to date version of LUKS is a good one to use and is offered during installation of Tor in most cases.

➤ Your computer needs to be kept up to date in order to us Tor. That way you can build your workstations and avoid any security breaches. Try and check for updates at least once a day so that you do not miss anything that might update such as your security that is offered by your computer.

➤ Disable Flash, JavaScript, and Java. If you are looking at a site that requires these applications to be used, then it is advised that you look at another site. Should you absolutely need to go to that site, then you may enable scripting but it should only be temporary and done when there is no other option.

➤ Dump any data or cookies that a website is going to send to your computer. This has to be done by you because there is no application that is able to do this. So, you are going to get an add on that is going to be called self destructing cookies and that is going to make it to where any cookies on your computer are destroyed completely.

- ➢ It is wise to make your workstation a laptop because it can easily be moved and gotten rid of it there is a problem.

- ➢ Google, while a popular search engine, should not be used. Try and use a start up page instead so that you are not required to put in a captcha.

Along with how you use Tor, the environment in which you use Tor is equally important. As it will be discussed later, Tor has some big weaknesses that are going to easily be hacked so that someone can get into your computer and get the data that you are inputting into sites. But, there are some things that you can do that are going to ensure that you are making it harder for a hacker to get into your computer.

- ➢ Tor should not be used when you are home. No sensitive information should be done whenever Tor is being used at home, even if you are offline. There are computers that can be connected without you ever knowing. Therefore, if you are not using Tor at home, then you are not going to be tied to a location. If you are worried about advanced threats, then move your location when you are using Tor. But, if you are not worried about these threats, you can use Tor at home as long as you are not worried about the information you are putting online.

➢ Be careful with how much time you are on Tor in one location. Hackers can get within the same time period that you are on without you even knowing. So, if you are using a public network like McDonalds, a hacker can be there the next day waiting on you. In case you are really concerned about how much time you are spending on Tor in a single location, then do not be on it for more than twenty-four hours in that location. If you have used it at one location, do not go back. People are less likely to remember you if you have never gone back to a location after you have visited it, rather than if are there every day or even a couple times a week.

➢ Any activities that you are doing online that makes it to where you do not want to be tracked, leave your cell phone at home and on so that if you are being tracked, they believe that you are still at home. But, make sure that you let anyone who is going to try and get a hold of you where you are going and when you are going to be back so that they are not worried about you when you do not answer your phone.

Now that you know about what to do and not to do as far as your computer and your work space, what about mentally? It does not matter what you are doing, how you look at it mentally is going to play a big part on if it works or not. Some people are going to be afraid to use Tor because they think that they are doing something wrong or they use the email that they use every day when they are using Tor. Changing how you look at Tor is going to assist you in using it.

- ➤ When you are using Tor, you should create a virtual identity that is not going to be tied back to you. You are basically wanting to separate what you are doing on Tor from your real life.

- ➤ Create new accounts with your fake identity if you are using an internet service that is public, such as ones that are found in Starbucks. Do not mix up your virtual accounts and your real accounts. For example, if you have a new social media account with the fake email that you have made, then do not create anything else with a different email on that computer until you are on a secure network and in a different location.

- ➤ Do not do anything that is related to your fake accounts on Clearnet unless you have no other choice.

- ➤ If you need to make a call when you are using Tor, it is wise to have a prepaid phone that is not tied back to you. One can usually be purchased in the sTore and when you do purchase it, you should use cash to ensure that your name is not tied to that phone. Do not use a SIM card with this phone and do not activate it anywhere near your home. No one needs to know about the phone unless they know about your fake identity.

Using Tor also has its benefits such as hiding what you are doing online. There is an increase in privacy and security when you are using Tor. This can be especially helpful to make sure hackers or any government agencies are not seeing what you are doing. So, if you are doing things that you do not want tied back to you, Tor is going to be perfect for you to use.

While you are going to be able to hide what you are doing online, you need to be careful as to what you are doing and how you are doing it because you can cause people to become suspicious and they will watch you to see what you are doing. So, depending on what you are doing you can draw attention from family members or worse.

Chapter two

Using Tor to Be Anonymous Online

Chances are at this point in time you have already downloaded Tor. But, how is it that you are going to be able to use it? It is pretty simple to use Tor, but in this chapter, we are going to go over how to use Tor just in case you are not familiar with how to use a browser that you have downloaded. Not just that, but Tor is extremely different, so you are going to need to make sure that you are using it right and not leaking your information.

After the browser has been installed on your computer, there is going to be a folder that is labeled *Tor Browser*. Inside of that browser you are going to find that there is a button that says "Start Tor Browser.exe". You are going to want to click on that so that a new window is opened up.

From here you are going to be asked if you are going to want to connect to the Tor network or if you are going to want to configure the settings first. It is going to be best for you to just choose connect. It will take a few seconds before a browser is opened and will be connected to the network so that you are able to use the internet anonymously.

If you are wanting to ensure that you are connected to the network, you will need to go to the website www.whatismyip.com. This website is going to figure out where you are in the world based on your IP address. In being connected to the Tor network, your IP should show up anywhere that is not your actual location. In this case, you are connected and you are ready to use Tor.

Tor needs to be used for any browsing that you are not wanting anyone else to see. There are other programs on your computer that are not going to be connected to Tor so they are not going to be secure and if you are using them, your information is still out there for other people to see.

However, there are going to be some things that you need to remember when you are using Tor because just using it like any other browser is really not an option. Each site that you connect to needs to be through an encryption of SSL or TSL. If you are not using encrypted sites, then you are going to be letting anyone see what you are doing online as it leaves the exit node. There is a browser that can be added onto Tor that was made by the Electronic Frontier Foundation that will ensure that any sites that you are on are using SSL or TSL.

Be careful of where you are browsing. Just because no one can see what you are doing does not mean that you are completely invisible. You are still going to be able to get viruses and malware on your computer if you are not paying attention to what you are doing. You may be able to hide what you are doing by using Tor, but Tor is not going to be able to help protect you from something that may bring your computer down.

If you are not doing anything that is out of the normal when you are using the internet, then using Tor should not be a problem for you. It is going to be more than enough to help make sure that you are kept hidden online.

Chapter three

BROWSING THE INTERNET ANONYMOUSLY WITH TOR

People do not want others to know what they are doing online. Therefore, everyone wants to make sure that their online activities are kept private so that any searches that they do are not able to be traced back to them. But, let's be honest, it does not matter what you do online, it is going to all be connected back to you no matter what kind of WiFi network you are using. Things are going to be traced back to your computer and therefore to you. Many people are not doing anything illegal online, but it is hard to wrap our heads around the fact that we are not truly able to do what we are wanting to do online without someone seeing it. With as many people that are online, you can never really tell who is going to see what you are doing, whether it be a hacker or NSA.

Your IP address is going to be how all of your activity online is going to be traced back to you. The IP that is tagged to your computer is going to be a code that is unique to your devices and is going to be associated with any devices that are on a network. The provider is then going to be given with a geographical location of the device that is being used on their network. Each time that a website is accessed, that IP address is going to go through several servers which is going to put a location on where you are.

Normally the information that is sent through the servers is going to tell the website what needs to be displayed along with the advertisements that you see on the page. This information is going to be limited depending on where you are trying to access the website. Some websites are going to attract the attention of certain agencies such as pornographic sites.

But, never fear, there are going to be ways that you are going to be able to keep your activity from being tracked online.

The VPN or virtual private network is going to make it to where you are connected to the internet through a server that has a VPN provider. The information that is going through your devices with the VPN servers will be encrypted. The setup for a VPN will provide the privacy that most people need by concealing what they are doing online from the ISP and the government. But, it also enables the user to get away from anyone who might be censoring them wherever they are working.

You should create a geo-spoof so that you are able to get into services that you may be been denied before because of where you are located or if you are traveling outside of the country.

VPNs also protect against hackers when you are using public networks that way you are able to download P2P safely.

A subscription to VPN is going to be available to anyone on any device. All you are going to need to do is sign up with a company that has a plan that offers VPN access. Once you have signed up for the plan, the software needs to be downloaded so that all the applications that you are using are protected. A server location has to be chosen before you can connect to it. The VPN is going to hide the IP address that you are using and there will be an address assigned to you that is associated with the server that you are using. After that, the activity that you participate on online is going to be hidden as well as encrypted. You are going to be able to use your own network or public networks without anything being traced back to you.

When a VPN is chosen, you will look for features that are going to be important to your connectivity and the security that you are looking for. The VPN needs to have the proper bandwidth so that it can deal with any data transfer limits that may be set by the internet service provider. Most VPNs have unlimited bandwidth, but you need to double check and make sure that you are not getting one that has limits or your browsing is going to be slowed down.

The VPN should also allow for multiple devices to be connected at once.

Last but not last, you will want to look for how strong the encryption is. The two strengths that you are going to see the most are 128 and 256 bit. The bigger one is obviously going to be the stronger strength, so if you can, you will want to get that one. The VPN should also enable you to choose what security protocols are put into place. Encryption has the possibility of slowing down your network connection depending on how high it is set.

As you continue to search for VPN, you will also want to look at the network size. The VPN that you pick needs to have at least fifty servers on their network if not more. The more servers that there are, the wider the distribution is going to be so the higher the bandwidth will be.

Be sure that you check the compatibility of the system. Basically, all you are doing is making sure that it is going to work with the devices that you are using. VPNs with automatic set up and excellent customer service are going to be the ones that you are wanting to go with just in case you end up needing some help with it. Here are the top three VPNs that are going to make it easier for you to get around online without anyone knowing what you are doing.

➤ Express VPN: anyone who uses this VPN gave it a fairly high score. It has one of the highest encryptions that you are going to be able to get as well as a fast connection. There are some pros and cons as there is with anything that you are going to use. Express has unlimited bandwidth and you are able to get at least two connections per account. There is a worldwide network available, automatic set up, and it is compatible with most of the devices that are used. Not only that, but the connection is fast and reliable. There is a 256 bit encryption plan and you can customize it to fit your needs. Along with that, you will be able to get help twenty four seven and if you are not happy with it, you will get your money back. Express however does not have any phone support, all the support that you are going to find is going to be online.

➤ IPVanish: with IP vanish, it got a relatively high rating, but not as high as Express. There is a fast connection and it will allow you to have two connections per account. There is also unlimited bandwidth available at a 256 bit encryption rate. The network is worldwide and there is twenty four seven support through email. If you do not like it, you have one week to be able to get your money back. It cannot be used with iOS though and there is no referral program. It may have great connectivity, but it is not going to be the best if you are an Apple user.

> HideMyAss: this is the last VPN that will be discussed. It too has unlimited bandwidth and is compatible with all devices. Just like the other ones you are able to get two connections per device and you are going to have 256 encryptions. There is twenty four hour support should you need it. But, the connection is going to be slow and at best, unreliable. The customer support is going to be slow to respond to anything that you ask and the software is going to make it to where you may find it difficult to use. So, it is not one of the best options for you to pick from for VPN.

There are going to be other VPNs that you can choose from so that you can hide what you are doing online. The decision is going to be up to you on what you decide to do.

Chapter four

EVADING THE NSA SO THEY CANNOT SPY ON YOU

The NSA is one of the government agencies that looks at what the people of the United States are doing on the internet so that they can try and catch terrorists. But, not everyone wants the NSA to know what they are doing online, especially the government because some people think that the government already has too much power and allowing them to know what is going on in our personal lives is to hide what we are doing so that we can protect ourselves.

A tool has been created by security researchers that allows for people to lower the chance of a bad Tor connection being used. These same researchers have said that the AsToria tool for Tor is made to beat any attacks that may occur on Tor.

American and Israeli researchers developed the AsToria tool to be able to provide the users of Tor a way to get rid of the autonomous systems that are constantly trying to reveal their online identities. Timed attacks are going to be one of the biggest threats that Astroia helps to prevent.

One of the researchers said: "Defeating timing attacks against Tor completely isn't possible because of how Tor is built, but making the attacks more costly and less likely to succeed is a pastime that Tor developers have dedicated a decade to. AsToria follows in those footsteps."

Algorithms have been built into AsToria so that they are able to fight against any of the worst case scenarios that may pop up. AsToria automatically checks to see which is the best route so that no relays become available.

AsToria is meant to be an add on for Tor so that you are able to continue to hide when you are online. The NSA and FBI want to take down Tor because it makes it to where they cannot watch everything that everyone is doing. If they are able to find any weakness that Tor might have, they are going to use it to try and exTort the connection, even if that means putting a virus on your computer.

Tor, if used properly, is going to hide what you are doing online as we have discussed earlier in this book. However, there are always going to be people or agencies that are going to try and get into the browser.

Even if you have AsToria added on to your browser and if you do everything that you know is going to protect you so that you are not going to be attacked, that does not mean that something is not going to happen.

Just forgetting to use Tor one time, using it in the wrong place, or going to the same place to use the network more than once is going to make it to where hackers such as the NSA are able to crack through all the security measures that you have in place and figure out what it is that you are doing.

A few other things that you can do is to quit social media. You do not have to go on and delete your profile if you do not want to, but you can stop logging in and posting on them. It does not matter what you post or if you try and delete it, once it is out there, it is there...for good.

Not only are you going to be stopping other various issues that social media can bring around, but you are going to be stopping the NSA from having access to what you are doing on social media but looking at the servers for that social media.

In all honesty, unless you have given the NSA something to worry about, you do not need to worry about them spying on you. They have better things to do with their time than to follow someone around on the internet who is using social media and their email.

The thing is, Tor is going to be the best way that you are going to be able to hide what you are doing online. Just be careful with what you are doing online and you should be fine and not have to worry about any viruses getting onto your computer or someone hacking it.

If you are that worried about the government keeping an eye on you, simply log off. Get off the computer and do not look back. If you are not on it, then how are they going to keep tabs on you?

Chapter five

USING TOR FOR HACKING

Hacking is done for many different reasons. Hacking is highly illegal and needs to be done under safe circumstances. You can use Tor to hack like you can any other application. But, there are more ways that you are going to be able to hack with Tor, it is just going to make it more complex and you will need to have more patience. Just like with any hacking, you are going to need to be diligent and make sure you are not going too fast or else you may get caught.

The most obvious first step is going to be that you need to download a Tor Browser. You can go to www.Torproject.org and find a download for the browser. Make sure that you set up your browser and configure it to the way that you are wanting it to be so that it works for you. The most common way to set up Tor is to just let it go through its normal set up. Settings can always be changed at a later date.

As we talked about earlier, you are going to want to test the Tor network and make sure that you are actually on the network. If you are not on the network, then you are going to get caught being that you are not going to be hiding very well because your IP address is going to be the same IP address that is tied to where you are. You do not want people to know where you are or you are going to lead them right to your front door!

Now you are going to enter deepweb.pw onto the Tor browser's URL bar. You now have access to the deep web services like: Hidden Wiki, Tails, Tor Search Engines and much more.

The hidden wiki is going to give deep web sites that you are going to be able to access when illegal business is being done. Please note that this book is not advocating anything that is illegal. The hacking purposes that are talked about in this book are for educational purposes only. Anything that is done illegally is going to be able to be persecuted under the full extent of the law if and when you get caught. So, it is not advised that you do anything illegal, even if no one can see what it is that you are doing online.

Congratulations, you are now in deep web.

With deep web you can use the tunnels that are associated with Tor to get into other websites.

However, you can also add on tools to a browser such as FireFox that are going to make hacking that much easier because not only are they going to hide what you are doing and where you are, but they are also going to make it to where you do not have as many steps to go through when you are trying to hack.

These two add ons are Page Hacker and HackBar. Both of these add ons will enable you to use traditional hacking skills needed to hack into systems and websites.

Here are the traditional steps that you may follow for hacking into a system. The only difference that you are going to see is that you are going to use Tor and the add ons that you now have.

Step One:

You're going to want to use a *nix terminal for all your commands that you're going to be using when it comes to hacking. Cygwin is a good program that will actually emulate the *nix for those users who use Windows. If you do not have access to Cygwin, then it is best that you use Nmap which will run off WinPCap while you're still on windows even though you're not using Cygwin. However, the downside to Nmap is that it will run poorly on the Windows operating system because there is a lack of raw sockets.

When you're actually hacking, you're most likely going to want to consider using BSD or Linux as both of these systems are flexible no matter what type of system you are using. But, it is important to know that Linux will have more tools that are pre-installed and ultimately more useful to you when it comes to your hacking ventures.

Step Two:

Make sure that the machine you are using to hack is actually secured. You're going to need to make sure that you are protected before you go hacking into anyone else's system. If you are not secured, then there is a possibility that you are going to be traced and they will be able to get ahold of you and even file a lawsuit against you because they now know where you are.

If you're hacking a system that is a friend, family members, or a companies, make sure that you do not do so without the permission of the system's owner. The permission needs to ultimately be handwritten so that there are no repercussions that can come back on you.

If you do not feel comfortable attacking someone else's system, then you always have the option of attacking your own system in order to find your own securities flaws. In order to do this, you'll need to set up a virtual laboraTory to hack.

Ultimately, it does not matter what you are trying to hack, if you do not have the permission of the administraTor, it is illegal and you will get in trouble.

Step Three:

You're going to want to make sure that you can reach the system in which you are trying to attack. You can use a ping utility tool in order to test and see if your target is active, however, the results from this cannot always be trusted. If you are using a ping utility tool, the biggest flaw you will find is that the system administraTor will actually be able to turn their system off and therefore causing you to lose your target.

Step Four:

You're going to need to run a scan of the ports on the system that you're trying to attack by using pOf or Nmap in order to check and see which ports are actually open on the machine. Along with telling you which ports are open, you'll also be able to see what type of firewall is being used as well as what kind of router is being used.

Knowing this type of information is going to help you to plot your course of action in attacking the system. In order to activate the OS detection using Nmap, you're going to use the -O switch.

Step Five:

Ports such as those that use HTTP or FTP are going to more often than not be protected ports and are only going to become unsecure and discoverable when they are exploited.

Ports that are left open for LAN gaming such as TCP and UDP are often forgotten much like the Telnet ports.

Any ports that are open are usually evidence of a SSH (secure shell service) that is running on your target. Sometimes these ports can be forced open with brute force in order to allow you access to them.

Step Six:

Before you are able to gain access to most systems, there is a password that you're going to have to crack. You are able to use brute force in order to crack the password as one of the ways that you can try and get into a system. When you use brute force, your effort of trying every possible password contained within a pre-defined dictionary is put onto a software program and used to try and crack the password.

Being that users of any website or system are highly discouraged from using passwords that are weak and easy to crack, sometimes using brute force can take some time in trying to crack a password. However, there have been some major improvements to the brute force techniques in an effort to lower the time that it takes to crack a password.

You can also improve your cracking speed by using cracking algorithms. Many hashing algorithms can be weak and therefore are exploited in using their weakness in order to easily gain access to the system that you are trying to attack.

For example, if you have an MD5 algorithm and cut it in 1/4, you will then have a huge boost in the speed used to crack the password.

Graphics cards are also now being used as another sort of processor that you can gain access to. Gaining access to a graphics card is a thousand times faster than it is to crack a password or use an algorithm in order to attack the system.

It is highly advised that you do not try and attempted every possible password option when you are trying to access a machine remotely. If you're going to use this technique, then you're more than likely going to be detected due to the pollution of the system logs and it will take years to complete.

When you're using an IP address to access a proxy, you're going to need to have a rooted tablet as well as install a program called TCP scan. The TCP will have a signal that will upload and allow you to gain access to the secure site that you're trying to attack.

In the end, when you look at it, the easiest way to gain access to any system is to find a way that does not require you to have to crack a password.

Step Seven:

If you're targeting a *nix machine, you're going to need to try and get the root privileges. When you're trying to gain access to a Windows system, you're going to need to get the administraTor privileges.

If you want to see all the files on the system, you're going to need to have super-user privileges. Having super user privileges allows you to have an account that will give you access as a root user in the Linux or BSD systems.

Even if you're wanting to have access to the most basic kinds of files on a computer, you're going to need to have some kind of privileges that will allow you to see the files. So, no matter what, if you're wanting to see anything on a computer, you're going to need to have some sort of privileges that will allow you to see what is on the network. These privileges will come from the system administraTor.

A system that uses a router will allow you to have access to the system by you using an admin account. The only reason that you would not be able to have access to it is if the router password has been changed by the router administraTor. If you're using a Windows operating system, then you're going to have to have access to the administraTor account.

Remember that if you gain access to the operating system, that does not mean that you will have access to everything that is on the operating system. In order to have access to everything, you're going to need to have a root account, super user account, or an administraTor account.

Step Eight:

There are ways that you can create a buffer overflow so that you can then use in order to give yourself super user status. The buffer overflow is what allows the memory to dump therefore giving you access to inject a code or in order to perform a task that is on a higher level then what you are authorized to do.

Software that is bugged usually has a setuid bit set in the unix system. This system allows a program to execute a task as if it were a different user.

Once again it is important that you get the administraTors permission in writing before you begin to attack an insecure program on their operating system.

Step Nine:

You worked hard to get into the system, you're going to want to make sure that you do not use up as much time getting back out. The moment that you have access to a system that is an

SSH server, you will be able to create what is known as a back door so that you can gain access back to the system whenever you want without spending nearly as much time as you did the first time. A hacker that is experienced is more likely to have a back door in order to have a way in using complied software.

Step Ten:

It is vitally important that you do not allow the system administraTor to know that you got into their system and that it has been compromised. The way that you can ensure that they do not know is to not make any changes to the website or create more files than what you're going to need to create. You also should not create any additional users or you're going to instantly send up a red flag to the administraTor.

If you are using a patched serve such as an SSHD server, you're going to need to code your password so that no one can log in using that password. If they happen to log in with that password, they will then have access that they should not have and they will have access to crucial information that you're most likely not going to want them to have access to.

Chapter six

TYPES OF HACKING

You already know that hacking is illegal. People who hack illegally are normally going after someone or something and doing harm in the long run. But, there are other types of hacking or even hackers that you are going to find with Tor and any other programming language that is out there.

Illegal hacking with Tor is going to be just like hacking with any other program, you are going to be do something such as getting into someone's personal information or even trying to get into a government agencies. Many illegal hackers are going to use hacking so that they can get into people's bank accounts or social media accounts.

Sometimes they know the person, sometimes they do not. That is not always the reason behind why someone gets hacked. Hacking does not just mean that social media accounts are at risk, but identities are too. Once someone has stolen another's identity, then they are free to do almost anything that they want with that person's name and other information that they have obtained.

Many times, credit cards are opened and charges are racked up to the point that the person whose name it is in cannot pay them. This also puts loved ones at risk because it is making it to where that person knows personal information about you and therefore they are able to target your family and friends then.

There are other types of hacking that can be done not only with regular hacking, but with Tor as well.

➢ Inside jobs: this is going to be when you are paid to do a job from the inside. For example, if you work for the government and are offered money or just want to be malicious, you are going to be able to get into things that other people cannot and leak secrets. By using Tor for this, you are going to be making sure that the government cannot see what it is that you are doing on their computers. However, chances are, that you will get caught because it is going to eventually come back to you. But, this is not limited to those who work in the government, this can be anyone who works for any sort of company.

➢ Rogue access points: the rogue access points are going to be access points for wireless connections that are easy for anyone to get into. They are a major weakness in any network and if they are found, need to be fixed before someone who can do any damage gets into the system.

➢ Back doors: a back door is going to be left open on purpose where a hacker can gain access time and time again. Sometimes there are backdoors that are not put there on purpose, but this is going to be because passwords are easily hacked or the network is not secured. With the help of a computerized searcher, back doors and any other weakness is going to be found and exploited by a hacker.

➢ Viruses and worms: a virus or a worm is going to be embedded in another program or in a website that a user is going to open and release. Tor makes it to where no one is going to know that you have embedded a virus or worm into something.

➢ Trojan horses: just like the actual Trojan horse, these malware attacks are going to be attached to something else, normally a download because the typical user does not pay attention to what they are doing when they are downloading from the internet. This is why it is so vitally important to pay attention to what you are doing because once a Trojan horse has been set onto a computer, the hacker has remote control of that device.

➢ Denial of service: if a hacker does not have internal access to a server, then they can use a DoS attack that is going to make it to where the server is flooded so that no one else can get onto it. This can be done by random emails being sent or other various things being done that are just going to take up the server's time so that it is either slow or unreachable.

Not everyone uses hacking for bad though. Some people use hacking for ethical reasons. These hackers are normally hired by companies or wealthy individuals who are trying to make sure that they have all the security that they need to ensure that other hackers cannot get a hold of their information.

An ethical hacker is going to use Tor not only to hide who they are and what they are doing online, but they are going to do the same job that any other ethical hacker is going to do. They are going to get into company mainframes and try and expose their weaknesses.

The whole purpose behind finding out the weaknesses in a system is so that they can be fixed therefore the system will become stronger and hackers are going to have a harder time getting into a system.

- Ethical hackers sometimes are ex hackers that have turned around and are using their skills to help others.

But, this is not always the case. There are classes that you are able to go through that are going to make you a legal ethical hacker. Not only that, but you need to have IT experience. It may seem like a lot of work, but it is going to help you land some good jobs when you are ready to get one.

- As mentioned at the beginning of the chapter, there are also different classes of hackers. Each class of hacker is going to either fall in as an ethical hacker or an illegal hacker.

- White hat hacker is someone who hacks for ethical reasons and does not do it for any malicious intent. These are the hackers who are normally hired by companies to try and find the weaknesses in their system.

- Black hat hacker: these hackers use their hacking skills for malicious intent. These are the hackers that make the general public scared of anyone who is able to hack.

- Grey hat hackers are going to be the ones who are going to be between white hat and black hat. They can either use what they can do to help others or harm them. It is going to depend on the individual and the situation that they are placed in when it comes to hacking.

Chapter seven

HACKING INTO THE TOR NETWORK

As you have learned in this book, Tor is used for keeping online activity hidden from other people. There are agencies both local and federal that are trying to get past the encryption protection that Tor offers its users so that the internet is once again de-anonymized. There is a large number of activists and even individuals that use Tor so that they can avoid the censorship that is put in place governements. In fact, the number of users who are trying to use a network that offers completely privacy has grown.

Government and Tor

There are governments all over the world that are spending whatever money they can to try and make it to where they can moniTor everything that occurs online. But, a Tor network is going to make it to where networks are hidden and therefore cannot be moniTored. The governments believe that the networks and other technologies that are like Tor are actually a cybercrime and are being abused by people who might be a threat to their government or their countries safety. However, there are organizations that believe that online freedom and privacy are supposed to be allowed and that moniToring what is happening online is not ethical or constitutional.

Russian government and Tor

The biggest reason that a war has been declared on networks that offer anonmity is because they think that Tor is going to be misused by those who are using it therefore they ar wanting to compromise the networks. But, the United States government is not the only one that is wanting to take Tor down. The Russian government also wants to try and crack the encryption that Tor offers for the same reasons.

The MVD in Russia is trying to see what it is going to take to obtain any information about those who are using Tor as well as the equpiment that is being used by Tor so that they are able to get past the encryption.

There are companies being hired so that the proper technology can be developed in order to allow the Russian government to crack the users of Tor and all the activities that they are on the network. In fact, they are offering a rather large reward for anyone who is able to create the technology that is going to crack into Tor and make it to where the users are identified and the data is decrypted.

Tor network exit nodes being spied on from Russia

A four month study was conducted by two researchers in Sweden to watch the exit nodes on Tor to try and find any sneaky behavior. It was observed that a Russian entity was watching the nodes that sat at the edge of the network to try and catch information. The whole purpose behind doing this was to try and moniTor the exits that are on Tor to try and get into the network and figure out who is using it.

Just like the technology that is being developed to break into Tor, there are researchers that are trying to expose the exit relays and document any action that they come across. There is a tool that has been designed known as an exit relay scanner that allows them to discover when an entity has appeared to show interest in someone's online traffic while probing at the exit relays.

There have been at least twenty-five nodes that have been tampered with and about nineteen of them were tampered with through a man in the middle attack.

The Tor network hides the users activity and exprience under a set of specific circumstances by boucning the data through an array of nodes before the web site that they are wanting to get on is actually displayed on their computer. Any website that they are trying to use is going to go through around a thousand different exit nodes.

There were two considerations that were found on the study of the exit nodes.

- ➤ The Tor nodes are being run by a voulenteer that is able to move their server at any time that they need to or even want to. So, just before they are figured out, they can take their server down and set it up somewhere else so that the search for that server has to start again.

- ➤ The traffic from a user is vulnrable as it is going through the exit nodes. Therefore the information is open for eavsdroppers to see and get ahold of.

The attacks on Tor by the Russian government are done because the technique that they were using before was too noticable. It is actually believed that there is a group of individuals that is completely responsible for the activity that is being done anonymously.

NSA and Tor

A whistleblower named Edward Snowden put a series of NSA documents that were classified so that the NSA could be exposed as to what they were really capable of when it came to de-anonymizing a miniscule fraction of people who use Tor, but this had to be done manually. The documents were not the whole scheme for what was being done inside of the NSA, but it was to allow for a small amount of people using Tor to actually get caught by the US Government.

In reality, the NSA is trying to do more than what we actually know when it comes to getting rid of the Tor network. They are attempting to us different methods to get into the network. They are even trying to run malicious software into the network through the nodes that are being used when a user is trying to get onto a website.

The released plan from the whistleblower indicates that the NSA is trying to:

- ➢ Trying to get into Tor on the nodes that it runs off of. The nodes are trying to be used so that the user of the node can be tracked by the data that is going through the node. This method requires that the knowledge of the way that the nodes work between the destination of the user and the user.

- ➢ Thre is a zero day vulnerability with the browser Firefox and the bundle Tor. In using this, the NSA is going to attempt to get the IP address of the user.

- ➢ The cookies that are used on the internet are trying to be tracked back to the users of Tor. This technique is actually quite effective with the Tor browser. Cookies are meant to help enhance the website for the user but it can also collect data from the user such as that person's IP address. However, cookies can be avoided by using different methods such as managing the cookies that are sTored on their machine. There is also a technique that allows the user to set the cookies as well as the cache to be deleted as soon as the machine is set down.

There was a report that was published about a platform called Xkeyscore that was bing used to try and compromise the Tor network. In this report, it was stated that there were two Tor servers that had been targeted by the US intelligence. This was the first time that the source code for this platform was released.

XkeyScore is one of the platforms that allows for a wide range of collection from th data that is passed online. This goes from the analyzing of data that is inside of emails all the way to the browsing hisTory that people have on their devices.

Even Faceboook is not secure. All an intelligency agent has to do is provide a user name along with a range of dates in order to have access to messages that are sent between users. XkeyScore does not require there to be any sort of warrant given in order to do this because all the tools needed are right there.

The source code that was published actually gives th NSA the ability to track down people who are not in the United States but have requested a bridge information through Tor via an email or even downloaded the TAILS operating system. This allows the NSA to track the IP address through the Tor DirecTory Authority which is a vital part of the networks backbone. Every hour there are updates sent to the authorities so that they can get any information that is going to be relayed through Tor.

Law enforcement, cybercrimes, and Tor

The government is not the only ones trying to shut down Tor, law enforcement is as well. They are trying to track down the users of Tor so that they can help prevent any activities that are going on that are considered to be illegal.

The FBI was able to compromise the Freedom Hosting – one of the most popular hidden service companies of Tor – during an investigation that they were doing on child pornography. There was a malicious script that the FBI took advantage of inside of the zero day on FireFox so that they were able to identifiy users of Tor.

The zero day was exploited on Firefox seventeen and Mozilla was able to confirm that was how they tracked the Tor users. The flaw in the browser was implanted through a cookie which was then used to point out who was using the server.

JavaScript is the bases for the entire exploit. There was a variable that was hidden into the window that was dubbed with the code name Magneto. This code was meant to look up the hostname and address of the user and then sent it back to the FBI's server. From there they FBI was able to locate the users real IP address and then find the user. This script would send the data back through a HTTP web request that was not inside of the Tor network.

Magneto was what brought down the twenty-eight year old that was operating Freedom Hosting.

Freedom Hosting was hosting an uncountable number of websites, most of them being used for illegal activities under the anonymity of the Tor network. In the beginning, Tor was used for illegal crimes to be commited such as the renting of hacking services, the selling of drugs and weapons, and money laundering.

Thanks to Freedom Hosting, they were offered a host of services that were going to assist in making their crimes easier to commit with Deep Web. It came about that the Freedom Hosting service was also home to over a hundred child pornography sites so that the users of Tor could have access to it without anyone knowing what they were doing.

Because the owner of Freedom Hosting knew that he was being watched, he did everything that he could to not only protect his assests but try and go on the run. On his computer th template for the United States passport and hologram star were found along with ways that he could get residency in another country in his attempts to try and hide.

There were documents that showed how the software can be sent through a browser in order to get information from a users machine and then be sent onto a server so that it can be analyzed by someone who knows what they are looking for. In doing this, the Tor network offers an extra layer of protection, but does not provide a completely bulletproof plan for online anonymity. It has been proven that Tor can be exploited by using just the flaws that are found in the protocol or in an application that is being used to access Tor, such as the browser itself.

Breaking the Tor network with $3000

While many people think that they are going to have to spend a lot of money and resources in order to hack the Tor network and de-anonymize it, experts in the security field have started to find new ways that they are going to be able to compromise the network without using too much money or resources that are at their disposal.

There were two hackers by the names of Alexander Volynkin and Michael McCord that proved that there was an easier way to de-anonymize Tor users. The two hackers were planning on releasing their finding at the Black Hat conference that year, but it did not take long for them to decide that they were not going to speak at the conference.

A principal technologist with the American Civil Liberties Union thinks that the research that is being done on Tor and the fact that they are trying to get into the Tor network is going to caus a criminal to come back and sue them due to illgal moniToring of the data that is leaving the network.

It has been proven that it is not going to take a large budget or even for you to be the NSA to actually get into the Tor network and de-anonymize the users. It can be done on a budget as little as $3000.

Chapter eight

THE WEAKNESSES OF TOR

While Tor seems like it is perfect, there are some weaknesses that are going to cause it to have boundaries. Tor is going to give the protection that is needed against traffic analysis, but it is not going to prevent the confirmation of traffic.

Let's look at the weaknesses of Tor so that before you start using it, you are aware of what they are.

Eavesdropping

Autonomous system

AS is goig to be on path segments that are for the entry and exit relay for the destination website. AS will make it to where traffic on these segments are going to interfear with communication between the user and the destination.

Exit node eavesdropping

It has been shown that even if someone is using Tor, their usernames and even their passwords can be intercepted just by watching the exit nodes of Tor where the data comes out.

Tor does not have the ability to encrypt anything that is going through the exit node because there is no end to end encryption that is put into place.

This is not going to break the anonymity of the network, but, it makes it easier for authorities to watch the exit nodes and get information that can be used to figure out where the user is located so that they can be caught.

Traffic analysis attack

Advrsaries are only going to get a small look at the traffic on the Tor ntwork when they figure out which nodes that they need to watch in order to get the information for it. Using this attack makes it easier for people to lose their anonymity. It has also shown that the true identity of the usr can be revealed with this technique.

Exit nod push

When someone is operating a site they have the option to deny data from going through the nodes or they can reduce it for the users of the network. For example, you are not going to be able to edit websites such as Wikipedia if you are using Tor because an IP address is needed and the website has an application that blocks Tor up until an exception has been made.

Bad apple attack

Researchers have found that an attack can be made so that the users IP address is revealed if they are using BitTorrent while on the the Tor network. This attack known as the bad apple makes it to where the design of Tor is taken advantage of while looking at an application that is insecure thati s being used while a secur application is being used with the IP address of the user. The attack is going to depend on the control of the exit node or the tracker's responses. Sometimes there are going to need to be secondary attacks in order to fully exploit the network.

Exposing the IP address

People at the INRIA show that there is a dissimulation techniqu that is going to have the ability to get by anyone who is controlling the xit node. This study was constructed by studying six different nodes for around twenty three days. In those twenty three days, three different attacks were used to try and exploit the system.

BitTorrnt control messages

When a tracker performs a handshake, it is going to have the data that will have the real IP address of the user. The data that was collectd with this attack showed that around thirty three percent of the messages sent out had the physical address of the user.

Hijacking tracker's responses

Since there is no encryption or authentication when it comes to the data that is communicated between a tracker and a peer, there can asily be an attack that is known as man in the middl attack that is going to reveal the IP address of the peer while it is trying to verify the content that has to be distributed. With Tor, the only time that this is going to be usd is when there is tracker communication going on.

Distributed hash tables

A DHT attackis going to exploit the different connections that can be found througout the Tor network in order to figure out a users IP address. It is as simple as looking at the DHT despite the fact that the user is using Tor in order to connect to the peers of other servers.

In this technqiue, it was found that not only were other streams able to be identified, but they were also able to be intitated by a user who had already had their IP address revealed.

Sniper attack

When an attack is targeted at the node software, it is going to get the defenses that Tor has against any other type of attack that is going to be similar to it. There is going to be a bolluding client as well as a server that is going to go against the nodes until they have no choice but to run out of memory and are no longer of use to the client that set those nodes in place.

Heartbled bug

This bug is what caused the Tor network to be disrupted for several days in a row because the private keys that are used on the network had to be renewed. The Tor project sayd that the relay operaTors needed to be hidden so that it could stop any fresh keys from being generated once the open SSL was patched up. There are two different sets of keys that are inside the multi-hop design that Tor is set up on so that it makes it harder for Tor to be exploited with a single relay.

Mouse fingerprinting

In 2016 a security resarcher showed that inside of a lab, time measurement could identify the mouse movements of a user with the use of JavaScript. Each person uses their mouth different and it can be fingerprinted to make it to where you can tell where that user has been on the internet by using the fingerprinting that is unique to them despite the browser that they are using.

Conclusion

Thank for making it through to the end of *Tor*, let's hope it was informative and able to provide you with all of the tools you need to achieve your goals whatever it may be.

The next step is to download Tor and begin using it. You need to be careful using Tor because there are some downsides to Tor even though it seems like it is the best bet for making sure that you are completely protected when you are using the internet.

Tor can also be used for hacking purposes, and it is not going to be much different than when you are hacking through normal processes that are going to contain a nix terminal. The only difference is going to be that you are going to use Tor which is going to ensure that you are more hidden then you might have been before so it is going to make it harder for people to trace it back to you. Especially if you are not only using Tor and changing your IP address, but also if you are not anywhere that you go frequently or at your place of employment or home.

Finally, if you found this book useful in anyway, a review on Amazon is always appreciated!

Thank you and good luck